A Visit to the
Orchard

by Rosalyn Clark

BUMBA BOOKS™

LERNER PUBLICATIONS ◆ MINNEAPOLIS

Note to Educators:

Throughout this book, you'll find critical thinking questions. These can be used to engage young readers in thinking critically about the topic and in using the text and photos to do so.

Lerner Publications Company
A division of Lerner Publishing Group, Inc.
241 First Avenue North
Minneapolis, MN 55401 USA

For reading levels and more information, look up this title at www.lernerbooks.com.

Library of Congress Cataloging-in-Publication Data

Names: Clark, Rosalyn, 1990–
Title: A visit to the orchard / by Rosalyn Clark.
Description: Minneapolis : Lerner Publications, [2018] | Series: Bumba books. Places we go | Audience: Age 4–7. | Audience: K to grade 3. | Includes bibliographical references and index.
Identifiers: LCCN 2016049261 (print) | LCCN 2017001782 (ebook) | ISBN 9781512433753 (lb : alk. paper) | ISBN 9781512455656 (pb : alk. paper) | ISBN 9781512450477 (eb pdf)
Subjects: LCSH: Apples—Juvenile literature. | Orchards—Juvenile literature.
Classification: LCC SB363 .C53 2018 (print) | LCC SB363 (ebook) | DDC 634/.11—dc23

LC record available at https://lccn.loc.gov/2016049261

Manufactured in the United States of America
1—CG—7/15/17

LERNER
e
SOURCE

Expand learning beyond the printed book. Download free, complementary educational resources for this book from our website, www.lerneresource.com.

Table of Contents

Contents

Time for a Field Trip

It is a fall day.

We are going on a field trip!

We are visiting an orchard.

We see rows of apple trees.

Why do you think apple trees are planted in rows?

7

Many apples are bright red.

They are ready to pick.

We pick apples.

Our teacher gets a basket.

We will fill it with apples.

We eat some of the apples.

They are a tasty snack!

What other
kinds of apple snacks
do you think are at
an orchard?

The orchard has pumpkins too.

Pumpkins grow from the ground.

Look at that big pumpkin!

What other things might you see at an orchard?

There is a corn maze.

The corn is tall.

We find our way through

the maze.

Now it is time for a hayride.

We sit in a trailer.

Everyone sits on a hay bale.

A tractor pulls the trailer.

There are many things to see and eat at an orchard!

Would you like to visit an orchard?

What to See at an Orchard

pumpkins

apples

corn

apple tree

Picture Glossary

bale

a large, pressed bundle of something, such as hay or straw

hayride

a ride in a trailer full of hay that is pulled by a tractor

maze

a system of paths that people try to find their way out of

rows

things arranged in straight lines

23

Read More

Berger, Melvin, and Gilda Berger. *Visit to an Apple Orchard.* New York: Scholastic, 2012.

Lindeen, Mary. *I Eat Apples in Fall.* Minneapolis: Lerner Publications, 2017.

Rustad, Martha E. H. *Fall Apples: Crisp and Juicy.* Minneapolis: Millbrook Press, 2012.

Index

Photo Credits